The FOUR Fundamentals
of Practical Leadership

by

Charlie Logsdon

Copyright © 2013 **Charlie Logsdon**

All rights reserved.

ISBN: 148265931X

ISBN 13: 9781482659313

Acknowledgements

I would like to express heartfelt thanks to the following people for invaluable assistance, support, and encouragement in the creation of this book.

First I want to thank my wonderful wife, Margie, for listening to my rantings and ramblings about the need for better leadership and giving me her undying support during my continuing leadership journey and the creation of this book. Thanks also to my children Angie, Andy, and Lee for dutifully listening to Dad without appearing bored. Thanks to my brother Tony for being willing to read the manuscript and make improvement suggestions.

The endorsements from Alonzo Johnson, Lavena Wilkin, and Steve McSwain are really valuable. Thanks for the time you spent reading the book and creating thoughtful comments.

I thank all the bosses, Navy Petty Officers, Officers, pastors, and leaders of all the organizations I have ever been involved with. I have studied you keenly and learned much about what works and what doesn't when it comes to leadership. And, also, thanks to all the folks who had the courage to give me feedback about my leadership even when doing so was uncomfortable. You really helped me grow.

Thank You, Spirit, for the life journey that has inspired me to create this work.

Table of Contents

Introduction

The purpose of this book is to share a set of practical leadership principles that will assist readers in the development of their own leadership skills. These principles were developed during a thirty-year career as a frontline manager. Many of the lessons learned came the "hard way"—by trial and error. The errors were sometimes quite painful for all involved. A simple way to learn and remember the fundamental principles and actions of effective leadership would have shortened the time needed to develop good leadership skills. It would have reduced the pain and made the leadership journey more pleasant for all.

Misconceptions and myths about what makes great leaders abound. A popular misconception about leadership is that leaders are "natural born." While it is true that some personalities seem more disposed toward leadership than others and leaders start their leadership journey at varying skill levels, leadership can be learned and skills improved just like any other area of interest. Some of the leaders characterized as "natural born" leaders are charismatic and attract followers by power of personality and may or may not understand and practice the fundamentals of leadership. However, if they don't attend to leadership basics, it eventually shows as followers lose faith in them and begin to question their guidance.

This book is for the rest of us; those of us who have accepted a leadership position or find ourselves in one by default and realize that a base knowledge about leadership can help us get better results. Anyone can be a more effective leader if they are willing to learn the fundamentals of leadership and develop skills based on that knowledge.

As with most subjects, the discussion of leadership is complicated, especially if all its nuances are taken into consideration. Lifetimes are spent in the pursuit of knowledge of any subject. This book does not attempt to provide an exhaustive examination of leadership. Leaders in any environment would do well to continue to study the finer aspects of leadership. One can always improve. The purpose here is to teach practical leadership principals in an easy to remember format that will be of continuing use throughout the years.

The beginning leader can use these fundamentals throughout his life and can return to them again and again when things don't seem to be going the way he had hoped. The experienced leader can also use these fundamental lessons to examine his current efforts because fundamentals need to be in place, even when working for advanced leadership.

If the foundation begins to crumble, a house will slowly deteriorate and become very unsatisfactory. So, too, if fundamentals of leadership are no longer being practiced, organizational results can begin to deteriorate even though the leader is experienced and well intentioned. That is why high achievers in every area continue to pay attention to fundamentals even after they have achieved much success.

Larry Bird, the great NBA player could often be found in the gym alone practicing his shooting skills—even though he was already regarded as a great pro basketball player. He continued to focus on fundamentals. Robert Goulet, the great popular singer, was once asked how he managed to sing so well in to his seventies. He answered that he had always used a voice coach. You can be sure that coach often helped him refocus on singing fundamentals.

Carpenters must master the fundamentals of measuring, sawing, and hammering. Later if they discover poor-quality construction, it can sometimes be traced to inaccurate measurement, unskilled assembly, or out-of-square sawing. Accountants must master arithmetic but even CPAs find that basic computations are the source of misunderstanding and poor results. So it is with the fundamentals of leadership. They must not only be learned, but also maintained in a world full of distractions. The fundamentals of leadership as outlined in this book can be useful to both novice and experienced leaders.

The world sometimes seems rife with poor leadership. Anecdotes and complaints about bad bosses are regular coffee break and cocktail party conversations. Of course, some of this is because we have become a nation of complainers. However, much of it is well-founded. Bad bosses (poor leaders) are everywhere. Some indicators of poor leadership skills are: a heavy reliance on positional authority, not listening, only noticing the negative, not setting clear expectations or setting unrealistic expectations, taking people for granted... and the list can go on. A more subtle sign of poor leadership is a generally negative work environment. Of course, all the aforementioned negative attributes of a poor leader will *lead* to a negative work environment, and controlling the environment requires some particular actions that will be discussed within the framework of leadership fundamentals.

Poor leadership can have serious consequences. In his book about World War II, historical author Stephen Ambrose states that some of the U.S. Army leadership failures in the European Theater bordered on criminal negligence. Specifically, he recounts how newly arrived troops would be assigned to tank crews and be sent in to the field immediately. They often wouldn't survive the day. We will explain how that was clearly a leadership failure and how attention to the fundamentals of leadership could have prevented countless tragic deaths.

Of course, most leadership failures are not that dramatic. Some of the less dramatic consequences of poor leadership are: costly grievances and lawsuits in industry, lost workdays, high absenteeism and turnover, lost sales, and low productivity. Less apparent are lost opportunities for improvement. A workplace where leaders have created or allowed a negative, fearful environment restricts the flow of many really good ideas. Workers are afraid of criticism from leaders or peers, so they keep ideas to themselves and are less willing to be collaborative. We will examine how to create a positive psychological environment.

A leader sometimes needs to take action that is not apparently beneficial to individuals or groups, but may be necessary for the overall good. We will explain how to minimize the damage when such feedback or actions are required.

Since most people spend more time at work than nearly anywhere else, the quality of their life in general is greatly affected by the quality of their work life. In turn, work life is greatly impacted by the quality of workplace leadership. That is not to say that leaders have total responsibility for the quality of life of the followers. Obviously, many factors affect a person's quality of life. However, the leader does have responsibility for how the *workplace* affects the lives of followers.

Attention to the fundamentals of leadership can really improve results in any organization and can make a real difference in the lives of both the leaders and followers. Improved leadership can help to get work done more efficiently, thus maximizing the use of resources. This increased efficiency can benefit the organizations and the individuals directly involved and even benefit the society at large. It can save lives, especially in the military. Improved leadership, through attention to the fundamentals, can make an awesome difference in our world and individual lives. Besides making the world a better place, you can also realize personal benefits from greater job satisfaction and career advancement when you practice *The Four Fundamentals of Practical Leadership*.

"Servant-leadership is all about making the goals clear and then rolling your sleeves up and doing whatever it takes to help people win. In that situation, they don't work for you, you work for them."

—KEN BLANCHARD

CHAPTER 1

Facilitation

O

U

R

Make It Easy

F stands for *facilitation*. The basic idea of facilitating is to make an effort easier. So for a leader, facilitating means making what you want people to do easier. But, wait just a minute, you say! As a leader, isn't it your responsibility to get people to "work harder?" Well, yes, in high functioning organizations, people work with dedication and focus—another way of saying they "work hard"— and that is, of course, desirable. However, just asking, or even demanding, that people work hard is not enough to get the job done. A person can be cajoled, admonished, threatened, and even begged to do something, but that doesn't mean it will get done.

There may be some legitimate reasons that they are not performing as the leader wishes. One of the many reasons an employee or follower may not do what a leader wants is that he may not have what he needs to do it. Perhaps the employee cannot acquire something she needs to get the work done or maybe she doesn't even realize what she needs, whether it be materials, equipment, training, additional time, or other resources.

Great leaders can often see what the follower needs and make the way easier by providing access to the proper resources. For an illustration of how facilitation can affect results, let's look at a couple of real life cases when failing to facilitate caused problems and then, conversely, when the attention of a leader on facilitating resulted in improved performance.

Failure to Facilitate Has Tragic Consequences

The following historical example from World War II is recorded by Stephen Ambrose in his book, *The Victors: Eisenhower and His Boys.*

In the fall of 1944 and early 1945, as the North-West Europe Campaign raged on, replacement troops were pouring in to the European Theater of Operations. Many of these troops had received no training for the tasks they would be asked to perform.

An officer in the 3rd Armored "Spearhead" Division, Captain Cooper, reports a case in point. He got thirty-five replacements to help crew the seventeen new tanks the division had received. "These men had just unloaded from a boat in Antwerp a few hours earlier," Cooper said. "They had received no previous indoctrination on what they were to do." None of them had any previous experience with tanks. "Most of them had never even been in a tank or close to one," he explained. After they were given a brief orientation, the men were each allowed to fire the main gun three times. "This was all the training time permitted," Cooper remembered, because the guides came to take them to their various units.

The previous night, the thirty-five replacements had been in Antwerp. At 1500 hours they were on their way to the front. Two hours later, fifteen of the seventeen tanks were knocked out by the German tanks in a tragically lopsided rout.

2

Although lives likely would have been lost in the battles if the troops were trained and experienced, the loss was far greater because Army leadership did not provide any real training. They clearly failed to facilitate (make less difficult) the task of battling the German tanks by not providing the replacement troops with a basic necessity of combat: training. The newly arrived troops could not reasonably be expected to perform even marginally well at a task for which they had no training or skill. Of course, not all leadership failures are so dramatic. Many simply create ineffectiveness and low morale. Consider the following example from everyday work life.

The Undercover Boss and the Toilet Bowl Brush

A contemporary television show caught my attention simply by the name. It is called *Undercover Boss*. The show focuses on how high-level leaders of large corporations often have no clue how things work where the rubber hits the road, but the lessons learned apply to all levels of leadership. When the corporate leaders go undercover to actually do the work that produces the income for the corporation, they usually get a real wake-up call.

A recent episode was about an undercover boss at a fast food chain. She was introduced to a local trainer—a woman with over 25 years of experience at the local food production level. It became really interesting when the corporate leader was being trained to clean the restrooms. I don't suppose there is anyone who actually enjoys scrubbing public toilets, but it is a reality that someone has to do it. The trainer warned the woman before entering the restroom that it was going to smell and, judging by their reactions, it did. When the trainer said they needed to clean the toilet, the trainee undercover boss asked where the toilet brush was. The trainer responded that there wasn't one and they would simply use some towels to wipe the toilet and get out of there as fast they could (an example of low performance).

The incredulous undercover boss asked what happened to the bowl brush and the trainer said there hadn't been one for quite some time. So, instead of a proper cleaning, the restroom got a few quick swipes with some paper towels. It is easy to understand how this failure to facilitate by providing a basic tool not only affected customer retention when people decided not to return to the restaurant with the stinky, dirty restroom, but it also sent the message to the employees that management didn't care about them or the customers. I'm guessing some manager/leader got an unexpected tune-up when the corporate undercover boss got back to her regular job.

When Facilitation Works

In his excellent book on leadership, Get Your Ship Together, D. Michael Abrashoff, former commander of the USS Benfold, a billion-dollar U.S. Navy warship, reflects on his Navy career, stating, "I joined the officers' corps able to kick butt and take names with the best of them. But during

> "Time and experiences taught me what should have been obvious: if I didn't get the results I wanted, either I didn't clearly articulate what we were trying to do or I didn't provide the time, training or resources to do the job properly"
>
> **CAPTAIN D. MICHAEL ABRASHOFF**
> **COMMANDER USS BENFOLD**

16 years in jobs on land and sea, I gradually learned to stop shouting expletives and start asking questions. Time and experiences taught me what should have been obvious: if I didn't get the results I wanted, either *I didn't clearly articulate what we were trying to do or I didn't provide the time, training or resources to do the job properly*" (italics mine). To a large measure, because he had learned that it was his job to facilitate the work he wanted done, the USS Benfold transformed

from a dysfunctional vessel operated by a sullen, resentful group of sailors into an award winning Navy ship that provided an example of combat readiness for the entire Pacific Fleet—quite a different result from the example that Stephen Ambrose reported about the losses in the European Theater of World War II.

My Leadership Journey

My own leadership learning journey was similar to Captain Abrashoff's when in my early twenties I held a job as a production worker in a cooperage (whiskey barrel plant). Determined not to get stuck in a lifetime of factory assembly work, I began a program of self-development that included reading self-improvement books and associating with other folks who were seeking self-improvement. One of the results of this effort was an improved attitude toward work. I became a go-to guy for the foreman of whatever department that I happened to be working in. A strong work ethic, coupled with a willingness to communicate and work with the leaders of the plant, eventually led to an offer to train as a foreman. I accepted the job and the plan was for me to train on dayshift; then I was to be assigned to barrel assembly on a newly started second shift.

Unfortunately, the foreman I trained with was not interested in helping me succeed. He was afraid I was slated to become his replacement. The plant manager, Leonard, a real character who had been a moonshiner, union leader, and sawmill operator, saw what was happening, and reassigned the reluctant trainer, leaving me with essentially no training. I guess he thought no training was better than working with someone with a bad attitude.

Suddenly I was the boss of people who had only seen me as a congenial coworker before. Now I had to ask them to do things and take responsibility for their work. To say I was unprepared is an understatement.

Even though I had been a petty officer during a four year enlistment in the Navy, I really never had a group to lead. So, my preparation for leading mostly consisted of my experience with the leaders who had influenced me. Without the benefit of any real leadership training, I fell back on the leadership style that had made the greatest impression on me in the past. Unfortunately, the leaders who had left an indelible mark on me were mostly figures who relied heavily on positional authority to get people to do what they wanted. Fear was the tool often used to motivate their followers.

With only minimal leadership skills in my toolbox, I also relied heavily on authority to get the job done. That was a very difficult time for me and I'm sure I probably wasn't a very positive factor in the lives of most of my workers. But, I was no quitter. I was determined to tough it out, no matter what it took.

Like Captain Abrashoff, I could kick butt and take names with the best of them. I naively thought most of my job consisted of telling people what to do and then if they didn't do it, my first inclination was to think there was something wrong with them. They just weren't trying hard enough.

Of course, this led to many unpleasant confrontations. I just chalked it up to being part of the job. Yes, I was an asshole boss. As you can imagine, my results weren't stellar. I was definitely not a great facilitator. Although I would eventually get people the things they needed to do their work, it was often *after* they had been unable to get the work done. Only then would I realize that they didn't have what they needed to perform. I didn't really understand that it was fundamental to provide what they needed *when* they needed it. I left that plant at the first opportunity and moved on to another company. Fortunately, it was a corporation that did put more value on training.

Through that training, a great desire to do a better job, and the motivation of painful failures, I eventually learned that I needed to provide people with materials and equipment that worked right—in addition to the time, training, and environment they needed to get the job done. As a consequence, my results began to improve.

I focused more time on facilitation and less on how they just weren't getting the job done. During almost three decades as a leader in industry, I led production teams to many new production records. I helped to create a facility that was efficient, had a generally positive environment, was considered a good place to work, and produced continued growth.

Creating a place with such accomplishments required putting time and energy into facilitating and working to master the fundamentals of leadership. Of course, it's fine and true to say that facilitation is fundamental to leadership, but as with most things, the devil is in the details.

Seven Factors for Facilitation

How can a leader identify what employees need to do their best? Though it's different for various organizations, the areas for facilitating can be itemized as follows:

1. Materials
2. Equipment
3. Training
4. Time
5. Environment
6. Methods
7. Information

1. Materials – Or How to Make Silk Purses

Do followers have the materials to get the job done? Obviously this is paramount in any manufacturing operation. Although it applies to a lesser degree in office settings, people still need things like office supplies. It is also important to make sure the materials are high quality. You can't make a silk purse from a sow's ear.

I was in the consumer goods packaging industry for many years, and the quality of the packaging materials we used significantly impacted our productivity. When I left manufacturing, I made a gift to our newly hired continuous improvement manager of my largest file. It contained complaints to suppliers about the quality of goods they sent us with details about how the defective materials caused us problems. Poor quality materials were a constant complaint from production workers.

Early on, I frequently thought they were making the excuse of poor materials when actually it was unskilled work or lack of effort that was the problem. Sometimes I just thought they needed to work harder. Occasionally, that was the case, but as I learned to listen carefully and ask more questions, I came to understand that many complaints about materials were legitimate. If we are asking folks to make silk purses, then it is incumbent on us to acquire the best silk and thread we possibly can for them to work with.

2. Equipment – If It's Broke, Get It Fixed

Equipment that is suitable for the task and that functions correctly greatly enhances efforts to achieve objectives. For some organizations, that would be primarily computer systems. For others it might be industrial machines. For a lawn care business, trucks and trailers, good mowers, and weed eaters are needed. The military requires a vast array of equipment, including everything needed to support and protect human lives.

Each organization has different equipment requirements and the organizational leaders must take stock of what is needed and see that it is available in a timely fashion. An illustration of how an effective leader does this was relayed to me by one of my sons.

Andy and the Air Conditioner

Andy is a master automotive technician and one of the car systems he works on is the air conditioning. While working on the air conditioner of an old truck that I own, he became very frustrated because the air conditioner service machine owned by the dealership and used by all the techs had become very unreliable. The techs wasted a lot of time messing with the machine. Most auto techs are paid a specific amount for each job they do no matter how long it takes (it's called being on flat rate), so they are especially sensitive to anything that holds them up. Numerous complaints to the service manager had failed to get any action.

When a new service manager was hired, Andy only told him about the bad machine once— and he immediately sent it out for repairs. With one action to make it easier for the techs to do their jobs, this new leader increased the efficiency in the shop and gained the loyalty of my son.

All jobs have their frustrations and a leader can't create a perfect world, but when he can do something to help, it makes a big difference in results and morale. That service manager has since moved to a larger dealership, likely with a corresponding pay increase. It can confidently be said that the service manager's skill in facilitating helped him advance his career.

3. Training – If They Don't Know, They Can't Do

The story about the World War II recruits being sent into battle without any training clearly illustrates the importance of training. The need for training varies greatly depending on the nature of the work and the skill levels of the followers. Some folks are hired with skills sufficient to perform well. Even so, they will nearly always need some kind of training that is specific for an individual application.

Also, organizations have varying policies, procedures, and methods that must be understood in order for the individual to function effectively. In addition, people will typically need refresher training or training for new tasks, policy changes, and other changes that are continually occurring. New and improved technology and methods are constantly being created and will require ongoing education and training. Often this needs to be done internally. Perhaps encouragement to get further training outside work is appropriate. Many companies now offer tuition assistance to employees to help them improve their skills.

The quality of the training, along with other aspects of leadership, *will* affect the results. There is wide variety in training methods. Examples include "the buddy system," written formal training programs, combination programs that provide both formal structure and one-to-one interaction with an experienced person, and now online training.

Formal, written training programs with one-to-one follow up yield the best results. This allows the training to be created mentally first, then reviewed and edited to make sure essential points are adequately covered, and it provides opportunities for questions. It incorporates the four fundamentals of training; explanation, demonstration, application, and follow-up. More informal on-the-job training is used by many organizations and this type of training can be effective if it is structured to ensure that important information and practices are thoroughly covered and trainees are given opportunities for skill development. However, just asking someone who knows how to do something to train another to do it can yield poor results, because the trainer may be great at what they do, but may not possess the communication and organizational skills to transfer their knowledge to others. This sort of training is often referred to as "the buddy system."

Unfortunately, the trainee only receives training that is equal to the knowledge and training skill of the buddy. Some self-starters and those who are motivated to seek out all the knowledge they need for the job will do okay with the buddy system, but others with less assertive personalities may receive woefully inadequate training.

Whatever training method is used by an organization, determining the efficacy of the training is the responsibility of the leader. Did the person learn what he needs to know to get the job done? Some method of assessment is needed. This could include written testing, skill demonstration, or a combination.

4. Time – It's a Resource

Time is a resource like any other and a leader must make sure that when they ask someone to do something, the person has the time available to do it. I was once asked to work on a comprehensive training program by the training manager of a plant where I worked. It was an effort that would have required many hours of focused attention. The training manager was not my direct boss. He was, however, a leader who was tasked with leading the training efforts throughout the plant. After some time, it became apparent that my real boss, the operations department manager, wanted me to spend my time on her priorities and there was no time left in my workday for the new training program. This resulted in an eventual confrontation between me and the training manager when I told him he didn't have the authority needed to get the training program done (because he couldn't give me the time). Even though this occurred with someone other than my boss, it often occurs in direct reporting relationships, too. A better leader would have made sure that the time was available by working with my boss.

Sometimes the amount of time needed is difficult to foresee, especially when new tasks are involved. That is one reason that a good working relationship is vital to high performance. If a follower begins to see that more time is required than originally thought, he can feel free to talk with the leader about it. Of course, it can be tricky for a leader to know when they are asking someone to do something they really don't have time for, because "I don't have time to do that," is sometimes offered as a reason for not performing when the real reason is something else. Maybe they really don't have time, or maybe they are afraid to tackle the task. Maybe they see no need to take on more because they don't perceive any benefit to them by doing it. There exists a host of reasons why people don't do what they are asked. In 2007, Ferdinand Fournies published an entire book about this subject titled, *Why Employees Don't Do What They're Supposed To and What You Can Do About It*. In the end, though, it is the responsibility of the leader to make sure followers have the resources needed to get the work done—including time.

5. Environment – Creating the Right (Friendly) Atmosphere

An appropriate physical and psychological environment is required to get the best efforts from people. It is easy to understand that the right physical environment is needed. Often, the nature of the industry dictates a certain environment. For manufacturing, a factory is needed. Office work requires an office setting, etc. Most leaders seem to get this idea. What about the facilities that are provided for the followers' personal needs? If the restrooms are not maintained, no break area is provided, or the facilities are just not maintained, it has a definite psychological effect. Employees can easily rationalize that the leaders don't care about them, so why should they care about the organization? The psychological environment has other aspects as well. An environment can be dominated by fear and mistrust or by positive people interactions and trust.

Leaders definitely set the tone when it comes to the psychological safety of the workplace. Fear can be a powerful motivator and the temptation for leaders to use fear for short-term results can be great, especially if their job security or pay is tied to short-term results. However, using fear as a motivational technique has negative effects that limit positive results for the long term. Scared people are not generally risk takers. An organization where people are afraid to try something new that might make things better will miss many improvement opportunities. Fear in the workplace can greatly dampen creativity. In his book, *Good Boss, Bad Boss*, Robert Sullivan said, "Psychological safety is the key to creating a workplace where people can be confident enough to act without undue fear of being ridiculed, punished, or fired and be humble enough to openly doubt what is believed and done." Some personality types will shut down pretty quickly when exposed to disrespectful criticism or ridicule. Others will begin to divert energies to plotting revenge. I have seen this played out in employee involvement team meetings, staff meetings, and many other settings. William Edwards Deming, the creator of the Total Quality Management philosophy and management system that transformed Japanese production, adopted as one of his fourteen principles - "Drive Fear from the Workplace."

Abusive bosses who use fear as a motivator are only one source of fear in the workplace. Employees will use fear to control one another too.

> "No passion so effectually robs the mind of all its powers of acting and reasoning as fear."
>
> **EDMUND BURKE**

At worst, employees will bully other employees by direct threats. More often, though, the intimidation is more subtle. Of course, certain kinds of harassment are prohibited by law and all leaders must know how to recognize illegal harassment and protect workers and the organization from its consequences. Other kinds of psychological attacks that create fear are not illegal but need to be addressed by the leader to create a safe psychological environment. Let me recount an incident when I was required to take swift action to maintain a safe psychological environment.

I once supervised several production lines and the lines were in very close proximity to each other. Employees could see what was happening on adjacent lines and often would help each other out. However, the help wasn't always appreciated. An employee on one of the lines saw defective product going past the inspector on another line. She called out to the inspector about the defective product, knowing the inspector was distracted and the defective product was likely going to get out of the plant. The inspector immediately responded by shouting abusively to her coworker with accompanying expletives that she needed to "mind her own business." I was in earshot and heard and saw the exchange. I quickly removed the abuser from the line and brought her to the office where I made it clear that the behavior was unacceptable. This particular employee was emotionally unstable and I knew that it was not going to be pretty. I was right. She vacillated between sobbing and telling me to "bring it on." Outside the office, my boss was frantically searching for the union steward and when she found the steward, she told him to get in there because I was about to fire the employee. I had no intention of firing her, but I knew I had to let her know she could not behave like that. I did give her a warning that was entered into her personnel file. That action helped not only the one person who was being accosted, but also let other employees know they could point out process problems without fear of reprisal from coworkers. Of course, a leader cannot stop all undesirable human behavior in the workplace, but whenever an opportunity presents itself, she must work to maintain a psychologically safe environment where employees can feel free to express ideas or to question others, even people in authority. Captain Abrashoff would have an after action meeting where even the lowest ranking sailor was free to question actions and decisions of even the Captain. Abrashoff didn't want to miss any improvement opportunities.

FOuR FUNdamentals

Another component of the psychological environment is fun. Organizations are socio-technical environments, and while it is essential to focus on getting things done, human beings are not machines and they always bring their humanness to the table. People don't live to work, they work to live. Having some fun helps relief the stress that builds when tackling difficult problems and keeps folks from thinking they are just being used like a tool. A good clean joke or gentle banter helps to create a pleasant environment. Laughing is good medicine. I once started a "Hawaiian Shirt Day." On Fridays I wore Hawaiian shirts (we were in Kentucky) and others started wearing them too. It was fun to see everyone in aloha shirts as if we were all on vacation. Potluck dinners, company picnics, and many other activities can be provided to let folks have some fun and let them know they are valued. While practicing the Four Fundamentals of Practical Leadership, don't forget to have some fun.

> "Against the assault of laughter nothing can stand."
>
> **MARK TWAIN, THE MYSTERIOUS STRANGER**

6. Methods

Tasks can often be made easier by formalizing the methods to be used. Formal methods can be Standard Operating Procedures (SOPs), GMPs (Good Manufacturing Practices), checklists, forms, software programs, or any other standardized methods that make routine tasks easier. It is critical that some tasks proceed according to specific sequenced action steps. Who would want to get on an airplane without knowing the crew had used a detailed checklist to make sure the plane was ready to take off? Although these formal methods of accomplishing tasks may be born of the necessity to ensure quality, they are an important form of facilitation because they also make it easier for the employee to do his work efficiently and confidently. A great way to accomplish this is to have followers involved in creating, modifying, and maintaining the methods. As self-improvement guru Stephen Covey says: "No involvement, no commitment." If folks can be involved in establishing work processes, they will be much more committed to using them. Of course, leaders also want followers to think about what they are doing and not just follow the methods without question. Unforeseen problems may cause a need for adjustments to the method and followers are in the best position to react appropriately or give feedback about needed changes.

7. Information – It's Powerful

It is more important than ever that leaders provide the information necessary for followers to accomplish their jobs. Nearly all jobs are becoming more complex and the ever-increasing pace of change requires quick decision making and action. Customer requirements, work techniques, regulatory requirements, etc., are in a constant state of flux. People must be equipped with the right information to make the right decisions.

Also, in an information vacuum, people will make up things to fill the void and what they make up is often neither positive nor correct. The informal "grapevine" is much more efficient at spreading information than the formal communication methods used by many organizations. Misinformation and the rumor mill can do more than just distract from focusing on the really important issues. It can cause people to make incorrect decisions that affect organizational performance. A leader needs to be aware of the grapevine and, if necessary, take steps to supplant false information with the truth.

Keeping employees up to date on changes that affect their job performance and their welfare is essential to both efficient task completion and keeping a psychologically safe environment. Sharing of information by the leaders of the organization is needed so that employees can avoid repeating mistakes, make appropriate decisions, and feel included. Everyone wants to be informed. An example of the importance of information sharing is when an accident or other serious error occurs. The leader must make sure that other employees who may be at risk understand how the accident or error occurred and what steps have been taken—or need to be taken—to prevent recurrence.

Policy and procedural changes must be clearly communicated. Really, anything that affects the followers' ability to perform should be included in ongoing communications.

Much of this communication can be accomplished in a group setting for efficiency. Daily meetings of short duration are often useful to keep everyone informed. Skillful meeting leading is essential to make sure these meetings are not time wasters and continue to be useful.

Don't Take on the Monkey

Facilitation is very important to effective leadership, but I must sound a note of caution. Sometimes people just don't want to do what you have asked them to do. Perhaps they think it too hard or there is some other underlying reason that leads them to perceive what you want them to do as a burden or "a monkey on their back." They may bring up all kinds of "reasons" that they can't perform as requested. A leader must use their own judgment to determine if the reason is valid or the follower is just using an excuse to get the monkey off his back. As an example, an employee may tell you he can't do what you asked because another person hasn't done something that needs to be done before he can do his part. Perhaps he will even indicate that you as a leader need to bring the other person to task. Then you find out he hasn't even talked with the other person about what he needs from them. He is trying to transfer the monkey to your back. If you get enough monkeys on your back, they will become so heavy and exasperating that *you* will become ineffective. Facilitating doesn't mean doing it for them. I sometimes had employees tell me they didn't have time to do what I asked them. That could be an attempt to transfer the monkey. Now I would need to decide the validity of the claim and hold them accountable. If I observed them socializing excessively or wasting time in other ways, then I would have to address the problem. A discussion might reveal some underlying reason they don't want to take on the task or may be an opportunity to clarify expectations. I will talk more about setting and resetting expectations in Chapter 3 on *Understanding*. Good judgment and being able to discern the difference between excuses and legitimate roadblocks to performance are skills a leader will need to develop.

Just remember, you don't want to be packing a bunch of monkeys around. You want a follower to "own" his performance.

Examples of Facilitation

Working Safely

If a leader asks workers to work safely, safe work doesn't necessarily follow, because the workers may not have what they need in terms of safe equipment, personal protective equipment, time, or training. Equipment that is not maintained properly is more likely to fail in unexpected ways, producing new hazards that the employee is not prepared for. If personal protective equipment is not available, then the follower can't use it. If unsafe shortcuts to save time and increase production are encouraged or allowed, then the employee will be subject to added risk. And finally, if they are not trained to use the equipment safely, then they can't work safely. It is the job of the leader to facilitate working safely by making sure these components are in place.

Office Production

In office settings where reports may be a part of someone's responsibility, they may not have all the resources they need to generate the report. Let's say information from another department is needed to complete the report. If the worker cannot get the information from the other department, then they can't do their job. When the leader is made aware of the situation, he can respond in several ways. He could say, "Well, stay on them and get what you need." That may be appropriate if he determines the worker hasn't put forth the needed effort to get info. However, it could be that the other department is not being cooperative. In that case it would be appropriate to facilitate by contacting the department head and discussing the need to acquire the information. Every business culture is different and a leader has to know when to facilitate and when to refuse to carry the monkey.

Facilitating for followers has sometimes been called servant leadership and that term is appropriate. The leader is serving the follower so the follower can serve the high calling of the organizational goals. A simple way to reflect on this fundamental is simply to ask, "Does the person or group have all they need to do what I have asked?"

"What's the use you learning to do right, when it's troublesome to do right and ain't no trouble to do wrong, and the wages is just the same?"

—**MARK TWAIN,** *The Adventures of Huckleberry Finn*

CHAPTER 2

F
Ownership
U
R

Why America Works

Ownership is a powerful motivating force. People will work hard to own things. The great American dream of owning a home is a good example of how ownership will motivate. The desire to own a home may motivate a person to work extra hours or defer spending on things like entertainment and restaurant meals in order to save for a down payment. Ownership also causes people to take better care of things. It is common knowledge that renters don't care for property with the same vigilance as owners. That's why damage deposits are required on rented homes, apartments, and equipment. The actual owner of the property is attempting to motivate the renter to care for the property as if he is the owner. Economist Thomas Sowell explains how ownership promotes responsibility in his book, *Basic Economics*, by shining a light on the failed communist system of the Soviet Union. He explained that one of the reasons farm output per acre was much lower in the Soviet Union compared to the United States was that the key element of ownership was missing from the system.

Professor Sowell described how farm equipment operators in the Soviet Union would enter a large field to plow and they would plow to the proper depth only as long as they could be observed from the edge of the field. After they were beyond the range where the managers could see the depth of the plowing, they would raise the plows to very shallow plowing depth so they could get done faster. It made no difference to them if the poorly plowed fields resulted in low yields. Their pay was the same no matter whether the crop was bountiful or sparse. The managers likewise did not benefit from high yields, so they had no incentive to closely monitor the workers. Farmers in the U.S., on the other hand, know that the higher the yield, the more money they make. Therefore, they accept responsibility for performance at each stage of the growing and harvesting process. If they do the work personally, they focus on doing it right so as to get the best yield. If they hire others to do the work, they monitor closely to ensure the work is done properly.

So it is easy to understand how ownership promotes good work practices and even innovation. If an owner finds a more efficient way to get something done, he will benefit. Conversely, withholding will occur if it represents a gain. The Russian farmer gained more leisure time by his shallow plowing.

Another example of how withholding may be viewed as being in a person's best interest is from right here in the United States. My father was a union worker in a factory. He possessed a strong work ethic, rarely missing work and I know he was a hard worker, because we worked together on many projects. It seemed when I was a boy, he was often laid off. Dad told me how once, at a time when he was very low in seniority and would be the first to be laid off in the event of workforce reduction, a new foreman asked him for any suggestions he might have for getting the work done more efficiently. Dad told me he wondered if the man thought him a fool. Dad knew that if the work could be done with fewer employees, he would be the first one laid off. There was nothing in it for him. He wouldn't get any more pay from his improvement ideas and he might suffer a loss of earnings. Gain or loss—whether perceived or real—will motivate folks to act or perhaps even to withhold. So, ownership motivates people to perform. However, it is clear that even in capitalist countries, not everyone owns a business and benefits directly in the successes of the business.

As a matter of fact, most people work for someone else, so they are not directly connected to the profitability of the company. In some smaller companies, employees may get a good feel for how financially stable the company is and realize that if things go bad for the owners, they may have to be let go, take a pay cut, or suffer some other undesirable consequence. Even so, most of the responsibility for profits falls on the owners since they will reap the most rewards. Large companies, however, typically have layers of management and levels of workers. The profitability of the company is obscured to most workers. The workers may not see a direct benefit of excellent performance in the form of greater compensation because they are earning a fixed hourly rate or they are on a salary.

Although cumulative low performance may result in the eventual demise of the enterprise with the resulting negative consequences to the workers, that fact is not much incentive to employees, because there is a disconnect. Many factors are out of the workers' control and the "big picture" is not easy to see. Like the uncaring workers in the Soviet Union, they may not believe good performance results in any gain to them personally. They also know that no matter how great their performance, the company may suffer an ill fate due to the general economy, changing demand, the low performance of others, or any of a host of other factors. They may feel like a little fish in a big ocean and can believe their work doesn't really have much effect on the long-term viability of the enterprise. Therefore, they may easily reason that, since they may not directly benefit from good performance and low performance will not result in any immediate consequence, maintaining a high work standard is not necessary. How is it, then, that large companies where workers may feel disconnected from the overall performance of the company often still get good, even great, results—even though the company owners (stockholders) are far removed from the actual work, as is the case with publicly held companies? Considering that employees may feel disconnected from the natural cumulative consequences of poor performance, we must consider how effective leaders control individual performance to ensure the organization remains competitive. They use "contrived consequences." In other words, they use a system of substitute rewards and punishments that will cause a gain or loss based on performance. People can then answer that age-old question: "What's in it for me?"

Contrived Consequences

Contrived consequences cause some gain or loss in place of the natural consequences. Since the natural consequences of poor individual and

> "In nature there are neither rewards nor punishments; there are consequences."
>
> **ROBERT GREEN INGERSOLL**

group performance are unacceptable, leaders contrive, or fabricate, various gains or losses that affect the followers more instantly and personally in order to motivate acceptable performance. These alternate consequences are used in every organized human endeavor to promote a sense of ownership. When we are children, our parents may punish us for crossing certain geographic boundaries. Perhaps we will lose privileges for infractions. They substitute the contrived consequence of the loss of privileges to protect us from the natural consequences of going into the street and being hit by a car, or perhaps when we are older from visiting a bad part of town. Parents also will reward their children for desirable performance, like offering material rewards for getting good grades because as children we don't understand the natural consequences of ignorance. Praise and criticism are also used as psychological consequences. These types of contrived consequences are not limited to parent/

child interactions. They are used in every area of life, including the military and business.

Drop and Give Me Fifty!

Think of the basic training drill sergeant shouting, "Give me fifty pushups, soldier!" when a soldier fails to assemble his rifle in an acceptable amount of time. The drill sergeant (leader) doesn't want the soldier to have to suffer the natural consequences of his inability to assemble the rifle when he is coming under enemy fire. He also wants to ensure the effectiveness of the entire unit by making sure individual soldiers perform well. Therefore, he uses the contrived consequence of the pushups to promote ownership of learning to assemble the rifle.

Business leaders also provide personal consequences in order to promote a sense of ownership in followers. These consequences can be positive to reinforce good performance or negative in an attempt to create a sense of loss. Performance appraisals are a way of promoting a sense of ownership. An overall positive appraisal is supposed to reinforce good performance and a lower than average appraisal is signaling that the follower needs to improve. A really good appraisal implies that one is eligible for a pay increase or possibly promotion. A bad appraisal implies potential loss of pay or position unless improvement occurs.

Incentive pay systems are designed to more directly provide a gain to an employee. Bonuses and piece rate pay allow employees to benefit more directly from their efforts even though they are not owners of the company. Various systems have their pros and cons, but they are examples of how leaders have attempted to promote ownership of performance through contrived consequences.

Discipline

Nearly every business that has more than just a few employees has some kind of disciplinary process. When an employee behaves in some way that is undesirable or some very low performance event occurs, the employee may be counseled or warned that such behavior or performance can lead to certain losses. The warning is usually finished off with a scary statement like, "Any further violations will result in further discipline up to and including discharge." Organizations have varying systems for discipline, but all have progressive steps that are related to the severity and/or frequency of the behavior or low performance. Attempting to intimidate another employee may result in a documented verbal warning, whereas punching another employee would result in immediate discharge. The idea is to let people know when they are headed the wrong way. Of course, a skillful leader uses this disciplinary process as a last resort. He gives employees feedback in an informal way that lets them know about their behavior and performance before things get out of hand.

Such punitive systems are used a lot in work settings where employees are insulated from losses such as demotions or pay cuts, yet still need to be given a sense of ownership. It places them under threat of loss if the poor performance continues. Of course, the purpose isn't to fire someone (firing is traumatic and hiring is expensive), but rather to get them to do better by helping them realize they may suffer loss unless performance improves. The loss could be tangible, like a pay cut, or intangible, like a lowered status due to demotion. People also respond to more subtle psychological losses and gains that promote a sense of ownership. A leader has a powerful influence in the lives of employees and must realize that every interaction with a follower has the potential to be negative (loss) or positive (gain). Here's a way to think about that.

Open an Emotional Bank Account with Followers

Best-selling author of *The 7 Habits of Highly Effective People*, Stephen Covey, talks about what he calls "the emotional bank account." It is like a bank account in that deposits and withdrawals may be made. Credible praise and thanks, compassion, little kindnesses and courtesies, sincere apologies, and standing by commitments all make emotional bank account deposits with people. Most people will respond favorably to credible praise or expressions of gratitude. A well-timed and credible compliment or thank-you is a powerful reinforcement. What do I mean by "credible praise"? If a leader says "good job" without eye contact while obviously in a hurry to do something more important, it might seem like a compliment the first few times, but then can seem insincere. This cursory compliment will be considered a platitude that the leader is using in an attempt to manipulate. The effect turns negative. However, if the leader says, "Good job, I noticed how you handled that irate customer and calmed her down. Thanks!" then that is a credible compliment because the follower realizes the leader actually noted something specific about her work and is appreciative.

Maintaining a positive emotional bank account balance is tremendously important. If the emotional bank account balance is high, then, when the time comes—and it certainly will—that the leader needs to give some negative feedback or does something that annoys the follower, the follower will be able to handle it and the leader won't become overdrawn, resulting in a poor working relationship. Leaders who build and maintain good working relationships tend to get a lot more done with less stress on everybody. Knowing that emotional bank account withdrawals are inevitable, to keep the account healthy, leaders must be keen to find occasions to make deposits. I would sometimes need to counsel employees when a mistake occurred due to inattention. Even though I would use my best communication skills to minimize the damage to their self-esteem, I realized that it would likely be viewed as a negative experience by the employee, so I also learned to be on the lookout for good performance and would let them know how much I appreciated it when they caught production problems quickly and saved the company time and money or contributed in other ways.

Looking for ways to make emotional bank account deposits with followers may require some extra effort and kind of a retraining for some leaders, but it is well worth the effort and will yield big returns in organizational performance as well as help create a much better work environment.

Continually making withdrawals by criticism, highlighting mistakes, or treating people disrespectfully will bankrupt the relationship and result in lower performance. Apply the overarching principle that has been taught for thousands of years: Do unto others as you would have them do to you. It is all too easy to get fixated on problems and forget to make emotional bank account deposits because some problems or mistakes can have some pretty serious consequences. It also seems there is a cultural bias toward focusing on the negative—the nightly news is a good example of that. However, from a leadership perspective, putting forth effort to find things that are right and letting people know you noticed their good performance will go far in creating loyal followers and getting high performance.

Awards are Great – Sometimes

Many organizations create awards to recognize good performance. One company I worked for had the "Chairman's You Can Make a Difference" Award. If someone noted something good you did, they could nominate you for the award. It was a big deal. The winners would be flown to the world headquarters in New York, wined and dined, given cash awards and plaques—all with great fanfare. I'm sure the recipients were glad to get the award, but I never heard anyone say, "I'm going to work real hard so I can get that award next year!" Those kinds of programs seem to get marginal results, although they do heighten awareness of performance.

A group reward system I once worked with was an 'excellent production' award. The company had numerous production lines and of course, it was desirable to maximize output and therefore cut production costs. Any line that ran production above a predetermined number of units during a regular shift would earn an award card. A new production record would earn each person three cards. The cards were about four by five inches in size, stated the accomplishment, thanked the employee, were signed by the department head, and had a nominal value of around four dollars. The cards could then be redeemed for branded merchandise that was ordered specifically for the plant like shirts, coffee mugs, umbrellas, etc. They could also be traded for gift certificates to various local merchants. This system seemed to have more effect than the grandiose scheme at the other plant. I believe it was because it combined a tangible gain with a psychological gain. People could hold the cards in their hand, accumulate them, and get a nice item. And, at the end of a day of production, it was a real symbol of achievement. "Hey, we got an award today— we must be doing well." It always amazed me how hard people would work when they perceived they could get that little blue card. Employees would help each other and really jump through hoops to get it.

I have touched on how important it is that followers have a sense of ownership about their performance and behavior. Some people will have an innate sense of ownership, some will have a generally good work ethic, and a few will have to be worked with a lot in order to get that sense of ownership. But it is critical to high performance that everyone understand that performance and behavior will have consequences to them personally. Helping followers to develop or maintain a sense of ownership through alternative consequences is a critical function of a leader and may very well be the hardest skill to apply because of the short term pain inflicted on the leader and the follower. It can be difficult to cause a loss to a follower, even if long term gain requires doing so. However, ethical leaders work to protect both followers and organizations from undesirable consequences. Long term gain can sometimes require short term pain. Viewed improperly, contrived consequences may seem to connote manipulation, but they are simply a form of influence that can prevent people from suffering natural consequences, which can be much graver and even life altering. Influence is what leaders do—they influence others. Whether they influence them for good or bad purposes is a different consideration. Contrived consequences have been and will continue to be used by leaders to get results.

Howie and The Old Moonshiner

In some cases, people do not understand the potential consequences of their performance or behavior, whether the consequences are natural or contrived and a leader may need to educate them. Let me tell you an early lesson I learned from an old moonshiner.

I was given my first opportunity at formal leadership in business when I was offered a chance to train as a foreman at a whiskey barrel making plant. The plant manager was a man named Leonard. Leonard had been the former union president and was infamous for having operated one of the largest illegal moonshine stills in a rural Kentucky county. (I mentioned him earlier in the first chapter.) I'll never forget the way Leonard educated a young man who I was having a problem with about potential loss.

As a foreman trainee I was assigned the worst department in the plant to supervise. It was the used barrel department where we received the emptied barrels from our parent distillery company and processed them in various ways. Although there was a core of employees that worked there regularly (some of them so they could access the dregs of bourbon from the used barrels), the department was also a sort of labor pool. When a foreman in another department had more manpower than he needed for the day, he would send his extra people to the used barrel department. The employees from these departments typically wouldn't like being sent to the used barrel department because it was the dirtiest and hardest work in the plant. Against this background we arrive at the story of a young man named Howie.

Howie was sent to me on a Friday morning along with a few others from various departments. Howie let everyone around him know he wasn't happy about working in the used barrel department. I pretty much ignored his whining, organized our work for the day, and gave Howie his assignment. All was good until Howie informed me a couple of hours later that he would be leaving at lunch. I asked him why he needed to leave and he said he was going on vacation and needed to get new tires on his car. Since it wasn't an emergency and his departure would have caused the planned work not to get done, I told him he couldn't leave. However, Howie did not accept my authority and told me he was leaving anyway.

As a foreman trainee with little supervisory skill or experience, I really didn't quite know what to do. So, when we took our morning break, I found Leonard and told him what was happening. He asked me where Howie was and I told him he was in the shithouse (that's the term all foremen used for the restroom there). It was a rough crowd of workers. Many of them were illiterate. Leonard said, "Go get Howie and bring him here." Leonard asked Howie why he wanted to leave and Howie told him. Some discussion ensued, but Howie insisted that he would leave. I could see Leonard was getting frustrated, but he resolved the dispute in a way that I have remembered for many years. Leonard's final words on the subject went like this: "This ain't no prison, son. I can't stop you from leaving. I can only stop you from coming back." I could have sworn I saw a light go on in Howie's head. In short order, Leonard handed Howie ownership of his job. The potential loss of his job caused Howie to think about the cost of having his way. Howie worked the day out. I heard years after I left the cooperage that Howie had moved on too, and had become a leader himself. Maybe the exchange that day was one of the things that helped Howie mature.

Helping followers understand and accept that their performance has real consequences to them personally creates a workplace where individuals take ownership of their performance. In turn, this cumulative sense of ownership raises the overall performance of the organization. A leader may be restricted in the use of monetary reward or punishment, but still can create this individual sense of ownership through the use of substitute gains and losses that include psychological and emotional rewards, discipline, low-cost group awards, recognition, and motivation particular to individual followers. Again, a system of gains and losses based on personal and group performance helps people answer that ever important question: "What's in it for me?"

"If you are a boss, your success depends on staying in tune with how others think, feel, and react to you."

—**DR. ROBERT SULLIVAN,** *Good Boss, Bad Boss*

CHAPTER 3

F
O
*U*nderstanding
R

The effectiveness of any organization is greatly impacted by the amount of understanding the leaders possess. Both cognitive understanding and emotional understanding are needed. Just imagine a ship at sea with a captain who does not understand weather, navigation, or how the ship functions. What's more, he can't comprehend what his crew tells him. The ship would surely be lost at sea due to his bad decisions. He just doesn't know enough to effectively guide the craft and crew. He is cognitively ignorant.

Now let's say the captain does understand the technical stuff about sailing, but he doesn't understand how the ship's officers and crew respond to orders, what makes them want to do what he says, and the crew doesn't believe he cares about them or their interests. The technical knowledge he possesses will be of little value if he doesn't have the cooperation of his crew because he doesn't understand them emotionally. Again, the ship and crew are in peril.

Understanding others and being understood both cognitively and emotionally are absolutely essential to being an effective leader. Influencing (leading) others requires at bare minimum that the follower understand what the leader wants him to do and is willing to comply. However, great leaders go much further to foster a high degree of both cognitive and emotional understanding with followers. The better the leader and follower understand each other, the higher the potential for achievement.

Of course, failure to comprehend cognitively and failure to understand emotional factors like feelings and motivations are highly interrelated. If a follower doesn't feel emotionally safe telling a leader something they may not want to hear, then they may withhold vital information that the leader really needs to make the best decisions or to grow as a leader. In worst cases followers may try to give the boss his comeuppance by practicing malicious obedience. That is when the follower complies with the orders of the boss knowing that what the boss has ordered is going to have negative consequences for the organization. To be an effective leader, promote open communication by creating emotional safety for those offering disagreement. You will both grow as a leader and make better decisions.

> "We find comfort among those who agree with us - growth among those who don't."
>
> **FRANK A. CLARK**

In the book, *Good Boss, Bad Boss*, Dr. Robert I. Sullivan, states, "If you are a boss, your success depends on staying in tune with how others think, feel, and react to you." Developing and maintaining a culture of open communication is vital to staying in tune and achieving the highest levels of cooperation and teamwork that a leader needs to move strongly toward organizational objectives. Since succeeding in our cooperative goals is so intrinsically tied to understanding, why is it that achieving understanding still seems to escape us much of the time? Because the sender and/or the receiver may not be skillful communicators, psychological barriers may exist, base knowledge of the subject may not be sufficient, or social and interpersonal skills may be lacking.

It is incumbent on leaders to take the initiative to overcome these barriers. Best-selling author Stephen Covey, in his highly popular book, *The 7 Habits of Highly Effective People*, says, "Seek first to understand and then to be understood." In his extensive study of what makes people successful, he found that focusing on understanding is one of a few principles that will really be helpful in being effective. But, he goes further by stating that seeking to understand the other *first* is the path to true understanding and effective communication. Being willing to understand first seems to lubricate the entire communication process. Everyone has a deep desire to be understood and when they begin to believe that

> **"Seek first to understand and then to be understood."**
>
> **DR STEPHEN COVEY**

a leader wants to understand them, they are much more willing to open up and build the relationship. This, in turn, creates effective teamwork.

Leadership guru and million copy-selling author John Maxwell declared, "They don't care how much you know until they know how much you care." If we seek first to understand, folks get an immediate sense that we do care. We at least care enough to listen and understand what they are telling us. So, if seeking first to understand and then to be understood is so helpful, why isn't it more widely practiced? It is often due to poor listening skills. Better listeners make better leaders. A leader can increase his influence dramatically by developing listening skills and being willing to understand *first*.

Another problem that inhibits effective communication is that we learn to block out communications that we don't deem valuable, to pretend to listen, and to fight to make our voice more important than others by all sorts of egoistic tricks—like interrupting—that shut down others' communications before we even have a chance to listen to them. Truthfully, in an ego-driven world, we may need to jockey for position sometimes to get heard. A leader, though, has to be careful not to let his ego get in the way of gaining the best understanding possible. There is a time to be heard and a time to listen. Here are some skill building tips for better listening and communication.

Clear the Landing Strip

Let's think of our mind as a landing strip for communications from the outside world. Someone launches a communication (a thought turned in to words) with a plan to land on our airstrip. When the thought vehicle arrives, though, there is no place to land. The airfield is busy with earlier arrivals that have not found a parking spot. On the sides of the vehicles there are names. Some of them are: *What's Next, What's He Up To, She's Cute* (a new arrival), and *Who's Watching?*

There are also: *Staff Meeting in Five!*, *Pick up Milk*, *What Will I Say Next?*, and many more. They are taxiing around trying to find parking or revving up their engines to launch. The new arrival can't find a clear runway to land on and so we miss the intended communication. The pilot of the new communication trying to land now has to decide whether to circle for another landing attempt. Maybe he will give up and go to another airfield. It is also possible he will run out of fuel after numerous attempts to land. If he fails to land, he may think twice before returning to that airport and may even warn others that they can't land there, resulting in other missed communications that may be very important to a leader.

To keep this from happening, a leader must resolve to clear a landing strip. That will require organizing the thought vehicles somehow to clear the runway. Some of them just need to "park it" until they can be directed to some useful purpose. Sometimes just thinking that *Right now what I need to do is "listen"* calms the other vehicles enough that they clear a path for the new communication. The idea is to let the message land. Organizational skills are very helpful in keeping the runway clear. To-do lists, planners, or any other organizational tools are very helpful.

Don't Be a Scriptwriter

Scriptwriters get to make up both parts of a dialogue—he said… and then she said… and then he said. It can make for great fiction. When trying to communicate effectively, though, anticipating what someone is going to say in advance can really get in the way of understanding. Someone who is scripting guesses what the other person is going to say and then works on a response before they hear the complete message.

A surefire way to notice this is when someone tries to finish your sentences. It can be a really frustrating experience because you start to think, "Hey this is my message, not yours!" While a scriptwriter is doing all this heavy fiction work, what the sender is saying is not getting through. I'm not saying that preparing for a meeting is wrong. Preparation for a meeting is, of course, useful. Just don't start thinking you know precisely what will be communicated.

The problem is that we cannot know for sure what the communication will be, so we cannot prepare a satisfactory response until we hear and understand. Focus attention on the message and then you have at least some of what you need to respond. But, you may not have all the information you need to understand and respond. Depending partly on the communication skill of the message sender, some effort to get more information may be needed before complete understanding can occur.

The Art of Questioning

Sometimes we fail to understand because we simply don't know the lingo that is being used or are unfamiliar with a concept. Maybe the person talking is not a great communicator and has left out some key information. Or, if a person is explaining something technical to us, we may not have the base knowledge necessary to fully understand what they are telling us. In order to understand, we may need to ask clarifying questions. One of the most far-reaching, globally influential leaders in human history, Jesus of Nazareth, said, "Seek and ye shall find." Skillful questioning is seeking to understand. We must be careful, though, to question in a manner that conveys that we simply need more information so we can understand.

Never give the impression that the person is being interrogated. Interrogation simply doesn't feel good to people. Note how uncomfortable people are on a witness stand. In a less coercive setting like a typical leader/follower exchange, they may just shut down or become defensive if they begin to doubt the motive of the questioner. That will not only interfere with understanding, but can have a very negative effect on the relationship, thus damaging future interactions. Even worse, if the ego of the questioner enlarges, questioning can be used to intimidate and even establish a pecking order by trying to prove some kind of superiority, greatly damaging the relationship.

Some good lead in questions to ask might be: "Let me see if I understand this correctly?" or; "Can you help me understand this?" Also helpful is: "I don't understand. Do you mind if I ask some clarifying questions?" Be aware of your body language and inflection. Even seemingly benign questions can seem like interrogation if your body language is negative or your voice conveys

> "Words are only painted fire; a look is the fire itself."
>
> **MARK TWAIN, A CONNECTICUT YANKEE IN KING ARTHUR'S COURT**

haughtiness or sarcasm. An example of the power of body language is when someone rolls their eyes as a response. Without saying a word, this powerful gesture can evoke spasms of anger because it is a form of disrespect. The eyes seem to have a power all their own.

Look 'Em in the Eye

Trust is built or destroyed by various ways, but a key element of effective leadership is trust. Secretary of State and high ranking army General Colin Powell proclaims that "trust" is the essence of leadership. John Maxwell, author of *The 21 Irrefutable Laws of Leadership*, declares "To build trust, a leader must exemplify competence, connection, and character." One way to give an impression of untrustworthiness to another person is to be unwilling to look them in the eye. I'm not talking about a prolonged gaze or stare. In our culture, these are normally reserved for lovers or used in an attempt to intimidate. But some eye contact conveys a sense of connection and trustworthiness. This, in turn, helps the person to lower their guard, promoting more honest and open communication. There is a reason we have a cultural cliché about a shifty-eyed person being untrustworthy.

Take the Time

It often seems that we just can't squeeze in everything we need or want to do in the time available. Meetings can be planned to allow enough time for quality communications, but impromptu communications which haven't been allotted any time at all often provide critical information. It is easy to shortchange these communications when we have other pressing duties. Extemporaneous communications can seem like an interruption in what we thought was a great and productive plan for using our time. If we appear anxious to get away, the follower can easily misinterpret our anxiety as a lack of regard for their message, and thus, them as a person. Again, not only can this cause us to miss a potentially important communication, but it can also have negative relationship repercussions. Of course, we do sometimes have more pressing matters that must be handled. If this is the case, then simply let the communicator know that you want to hear what they have to say, but you must take care of something really important right now. Ask if the conversation can be postponed. A terrible insult to most people is to abruptly end the exchange while someone is delivering a message. I once worked under a plant manager (I say worked *under* because I think that is how he thought of our relationship) who would simply walk away while I was talking. To say I was offended would be an understatement. When I finally found the courage to address this ill treatment, our relationship was greatly improved. Unfortunately, I believe we missed many opportunities to be more effective together before we came to an understanding about his behavior.

Another consideration is that extra time may be needed to achieve effective communication if a participant to the conversation is feeling emotional about the issue. A little ranting on their part may be needed before they can get to the crux of the matter. Just remember, they may be trying to tell you something that is going to be very helpful. You may not think the topic is very important, but *they do*. Of course, you can't let things get out of hand. Discernment is required to determine whether ranting is just about blowing off a little steam, or if it's actually becoming damaging to the relationship or general psychological environment. Very complex issues may also require extra time to allow for clarifying questions and checking for understanding. The real point is that quality communications take time, just like it takes time to create quality in the material world.

Open the Door – Let the Knowledge In

Followers can sense whether or not the leader is open to input. It is critical that leaders not restrict the free flow of information from followers. Using good listening skills, being empathetic, and being friendly are all key elements of creating an environment where followers who otherwise may not be comfortable with providing input and feedback feel free to do so, and these people may truly aid a leader in making the best decisions. Consider this example from my personal experience.

> "We build too many walls and not enough bridges."
>
> **ISAAC NEWTON**

I once had to administer a complicated overtime agreement in a plant with a strong union. The previous manager was forced to leave the company partly because he accrued so many costly grievances due to overtime crewing errors. An employee would be mistakenly awarded the overtime in violation of the binding contractual agreement and then later another person would have to be paid who should have been awarded the OT. Part of the reason that he got all the grievances was because he was arrogant. He was not receptive to any input from the employees about how he was doing his job. So, they would simply allow him to make overtime crewing mistakes and award the overtime to the wrong employee, even though they knew about the mistake in time to get it corrected. Then they would file a grievance to recoup their monetary losses. Each mistake could cost the company hundreds of dollars, all the time involved in handling the grievance, and generally gave credence to the oft used union claim of management incompetence.

Since I had been able to observe his demise, I put forth extra effort to be open about crewing the overtime. I probably knew the whole agreement better than almost all of the employees, but they knew enough to look out for their interests and consequently were keen to knowing whether they had missed out on a moneymaking opportunity. Since I worked to develop and maintain good relationships with them and was open to their input, they would tell me if I had made a crewing mistake before the overtime was actually worked so I could make corrections. Part of the reason they were helpful was that I had learned I needed their input and I worked to gain their trust. It was a wonderful learning experience for me and I learned a lot about being open, being respectful, and how to listen.

We Can't Know If We Don't Know

What I mean by that expression is that lack of the base knowledge necessary to truly understand can be a roadblock. An example would be when someone is trying to tell us something technical and they are an expert, but we are not. If it is important to understand the problem because you are a leader and ultimately may need to make a decision about allocating resources, etc., then extra effort may be required to upgrade your knowledge of the topic. It isn't necessary to achieve the expert level of understanding that every follower has regarding their responsibilities, but some knowledge is generally required. It can be a hindrance to leading someone if they think they are vastly superior in their knowledge of a subject and you are ignorant on the subject—or worse, you don't care to know.

A CEO, for instance, must be well versed in operations, accounting, marketing, logistics, and many other areas, even though she may not be an expert on any of the disciplines. A production supervisor must be knowledgeable about quality control, maintenance, accounting, human resources, computer software and hardware, etc., even though he may not be expert in any of these areas. Therefore, when accepting a leadership position, it is vital to assess the knowledge required and put forth the effort to learn. Followers will actually help you if you are humble. Most people are proud of what they can do and will willingly play the role of instructor if you are humble enough to let them.

Never Fake It

Pretend listening in some ways is worse than not listening at all. Pretend listening may cause the follower to take wrong action based on the belief that the leader is informed and approves. Additionally, if the follower recognizes the pretend listening, then the relationship is damaged because they feel disrespected. Pretend listening is characterized by sending signals like "Okay,

Alright, Yeah, and Uh-huh" while thinking of something else. Sometimes eye contact is very limited during pretend listening. And then there is that kind of glazed-over look in the eyes a person gets when thoughts have wandered away from the exchange. Pretend listening really isn't that hard to detect and can be very damaging to the trust and openness necessary for great communication. Legendary UCLA basketball coach John Wooden summed it up nicely when he said, "Listen to those under your supervision. Really listen. Don't act as if you are listening and let it go in one ear and out the other. Faking it is worse than doing nothing at all."

Bad Connections – "Can You Hear Me Now?"

Although seeking first to understand really enhances the entire communication process, we are still left with getting our message through to the one we are communicating with. Unfortunately, just shouting, "Can you hear me now?" doesn't work that well. As leaders, it's important that we realize that not everyone has good listening skills. Perhaps their work simply doesn't require the constant communication that is stock and trade for leaders. Even if they know that they need to understand, they may not realize they need to clear the landing strip in order to let your message land. Unfortunately, some folks seem to really struggle with this issue due to their own internal fears coming from their conditioning. The human mind is amazingly adept at creating complex defense mechanisms. These defense mechanisms can include looking for deception, projecting what the other may say and working up a response in advance, or simply letting the mind wander to other more pleasant pursuits instead of staying focused on the exchange. Therefore, a leader may need to work to improve the connection. Awareness of these psychological barriers to good communication can allow a leader to take steps to get past them and improve the connection.

The Man Who Talked to Himself

Emotional health affects both the desire and ability to understand. It has been said that we are all psychologically wounded, some worse than others. I once knew a man who talked to himself out loud much of the time. I had occasion to interact with this man often, as he was a member of my family. And though I cared about him, frankly, I would sometimes try to avoid him. Effective and meaningful conversations with him were difficult because he was so emotionally disturbed. His landing strip wasn't just busy with lots of traffic. Many vehicles had crashed and burned and were blocking the runway. He often couldn't take in what was being conveyed to him because he was too mentally unhealthy to focus on the message. His internal conversations seemed to block out much of what others were saying to him. Although this is an extreme case, it is important to realize that mental and emotional health can be an obstacle to effective communication. I do know that this man held a job in a factory for many years until he was forced to retire. I am sure some leaders in that factory had to use good communication skills to cut through all the barriers and help this man be productive and continue to be gainfully employed. Building trust becomes paramount in these relationships and some folks require an extra amount of attention from a leader before they can trust.

Friendliness and Respect

One way a leader can help people be more receptive to guidance is to treat them with friendliness and respect. Folks who are deeply psychologically wounded are usually very sensitive and are constantly reading others for danger signals. Therefore, it may be good to spend a little effort on making them feel more comfortable by engaging them in a very non-threatening manner and being careful not to give them reason to feel slighted. This seems almost to be common sense, but it is easy to get distracted and just walk by someone without saying good morning or acknowledging them. For the followers who are emotionally healthy, an occasional slip like this is not a big deal, but to those who are not as healthy, it may become a major sign of disrespect and a focal point for transference of hostility. Suddenly a leader who is seen as uncaring can be associated with the painful image of a parent, teacher, or other person who hurt them. The difference is that the follower is now an adult and they are just not going to stand for it—not a good formula for effective teamwork.

If the leader has perhaps had to deliver some negative performance feedback to a follower, it is more important than ever to be friendly. When I was a leader in a factory and something had transpired between me and an employee that I knew they thought of as a negative, I would go out of my way to come into contact with them again soon, while allowing for a "cooling off" period if necessary. I would observe them as I neared to pick up any body language cues. Sometimes, I could sense the hostility as I neared them. In that case, if no critical communication was necessary, I would at least greet them cordially. If they sent clues that they weren't ready for anything more, I would just go about my business and give them some emotional space. At least I had been proactive by "breaking the ice". If they responded positively, I might extend the conversation a bit. The idea was to bring the working relationship back to optimal as soon as possible. I would then treat them as if nothing had ever happened unless, of course, I came to realize that I had made a mistake. In that case, I would offer an apology.

Stephen Covey said we have an emotional bank account with everyone. We must work to keep a positive balance in our account. We can make deposits in many ways. Sincere compliments, credible thanks, learning what matters to them, general friendliness, and respect are all deposits. Sometimes, though, withdrawals occur. Perhaps we make a mistake that adversely affects them, or we simply must deliver an unpleasant message. If we have a healthy account, the withdrawal will not bankrupt the account. Look for ways to make deposits. Some folks will need extra deposits.

Check for Understanding

Sometimes people will indicate by verbal or nonverbal cues that they understand when in truth they don't. Maybe they are afraid they will appear unintelligent if they don't get it quickly. There is also the desire to be accommodating. Nodding may indicate that they really get it, but it also may be a habit they have developed in order to send a message that they are *receptive*—which is not the same as understanding. The only way to really know if they have understood what you communicated is to get them to tell you what they think you said. This is a tricky business. People can easily be offended if they feel that you don't think they are very smart. One way I have been successful in checking for understanding is to put the onus on myself. I will simply say something like, "I'm not sure I have done of a good job of communicating this issue. Can you help me by telling me what you think I was trying to say?" Checking for understanding is, of course, situational and will be impacted by how important the communication is and what the leader knows about the follower. As a leader gets to know people better, communication will flow better and checking for understanding will not be needed as often.

Setting Expectations

Followers need to understand what is expected of them. It is easy to assume that folks know what is expected. After all, they were hired to do a job and accepted the responsibilities of that job, didn't they? Well, that sounds good, but unless you as a leader hired them directly and have spent the requisite amount of time explaining expectations to them, it is difficult to know what they believe is acceptable and what isn't. Most people know that certain behaviors like violence or sleeping while on duty are unacceptable, and that they are expected to work. However, the productivity and work expectations can be nebulous to the new hire and are often subjective. For one, they may have received conflicting information.

Perhaps they worked for another leader in a different organization that didn't expect as much from them. And then there is the whole issue of formal rules and stated expectations that are not the reality of how things work in the organization. It is the leader's job to help people understand what he expects from them. Following is an example from my own experience.

"Tweeners"

In a plant where I was working as a supervisor of blue collar production workers, the labor agreement called for two 15-minute rest periods during an 8-hour shift, one in the first half of the shift and one in the last half. The employees worked on production lines where they couldn't just walk away, even if they had a real need. In this particular plant the practice was for people to take the contractual breaks and then to take another break between each formal break. That amounted to a break every hour. The non-contractual breaks were often referred to as "pee breaks" or sometimes as "tweeners," meaning in-between breaks. People do sometimes need time away from their job that isn't scheduled to take care of personal items like biological functions or pressing personal business, but the informal breaks had become an entitlement and people would use them to eat breakfast, visit with their friends, read the newspaper or comparable personal activities. I think this practice was initiated when many of the jobs were more labor intensive and unions were very strong during the 1960s and 1970s. Consequently, there was a clear disconnect between the formal rest period agreement and the actual practice. As a supervisor it was my job to enforce the contract and to minimize labor costs. As a leader, I had to find a way to bridge the gap between formal policies and actual practices, meeting the real needs of my people while keeping labor costs down. If I would have suddenly cracked down on all unauthorized breaks, entered people in to the disciplinary process, and attempted to eliminate all the extra breaks, I would have been perceived as an asshole boss and my people would have responded accordingly by withholding, malicious obedience, filing unwarranted grievances, and being generally uncooperative.

My answer was to set my own expectations. I decided to address any bad offenders. If I noticed someone abusing the pee breaks by staying away from their job too long, I would observe them more closely for a while to make sure I had it right. Then I would approach them in a manner where we could have a private conversation. I would tell them what I had observed and give them a chance to respond. I would then make sure they understood that the purpose of the extra break was to take care of necessary items only and abuses were unacceptable. That way the expectation was clear to them. A few times people didn't listen and I would have to enter them in to the disciplinary process. The point of this story, though, is that I had to set the expectation. That was my job.

Tell Them Twice

Some messages are worth repeating. There is a saying that repetition is the mother of retention. People tend to believe and remember what they hear, if they hear it enough. If a message is important, then repeating it helps make sure it gets through. This is particularly important if an entire group needs to get the message. You may not have time to take each individual aside, deliver the message to them, and then check for understanding. But, if you say it enough, the "grapevine" (the most effective communication network known to man) will even assist to get the message out. For example, if a new policy or rule is to be implemented, it is important to front a campaign to get the message out. Talk about it in group meetings and look for opportunities to talk about it in small groups or with individuals. Identify the informal leaders and be sure to let them know. You never want anyone to be able to use the excuse, "I didn't know!" If I repeated a communication to someone, I would sometimes have people say, "I know, you already told me." I would just reply, "Oh, okay. I wasn't sure if I had told you or not, but I would rather tell you twice than not let you know about this."

Different Strokes for Different Folks

Followers want and need to know what leaders expect from them. Although it seems reasonable that folks would understand general expectations, making assumptions can be dangerous. The diverse work groups that we enjoy today include people from various cultural backgrounds and experiences and many different generations within the varying groups. A leader need not be a sociologist to lead effectively, but understanding a little about the differences in groups can allow individual communications and interactions to be more effective. In some groups it is acceptable to be very direct in giving instructions. In others, a request to do something is more appreciated. Many workers who grew up here in the United States want to be asked something like, "Would you mind doing this for me?" Workers from other countries may be accustomed to a more direct style.

A lot has been written about the differences in how men and women communicate, so that is a consideration. Cross-generational workforces are also a factor. Dr. Morris Massey, a sociologist and producer of training videos states, "What you are is where you were when," suggesting that most people have locked in values from their formative years. It is very helpful for a leader to be cognizant of those values so he can understand what motivates the various groups. For example, people who were raised during the Great Depression have generally been very tuned in to financial security. Some effort spent learning about these various groups and their values will benefit a leader in communicating effectively and building that trust-based relationship that is essential to effectiveness. Consider the rapid growth of the Hispanic population in the United States. What are their primary values? Wouldn't it be helpful to know if you are leading them?

Understanding your followers both cognitively and emotionally is so critical to success for a leader that any efforts to improve communications and understanding will boost the influence of a leader dramatically. Emotional understanding sometimes gets especially shortchanged. We can get to thinking that if someone knows how to do what we want them to, they *will* do it. Highly effective leaders, though, know that a high level of both cognitive and emotional understanding is needed to work well with others and influence them toward high performance. Knowing this, great leaders become skilled at building a psychological environment that fosters open communications and relationships based on trust. Being proactive to seek first to understand and then to be understood sets the tone for their organizations. Creating this environment takes great skill and continual improvement. As with all skills, practice pays off. The sooner you begin to practice or improve the skills involved in understanding, the quicker you will become a more respected and influential leader.

"A good objective of leadership is to help those who are doing poorly to do well and to help those who are doing well to do even better."

—JIM ROHN

CHAPTER 4

F
O
U
Reward, Reset, or Release

A significant part of being a leader is evaluating the performance of followers and then acting to *reward* performance or get improvements. If all is well with a follower, they must be rewarded to maintain good performance. When improvement is needed, management must implement a review to determine whether the follower has all the resources they need to do what the leader wants. If they don't have what they need, including a clear understanding of what is expected, then the leader must determine if components of facilitation, ownership, or understanding were not in place and *reset* those components. If it is determined that the follower can't or won't do what is needed, then the leader must make an assignment change or separate the person from the organization. I call this *releasing* the follower. However, before any action is taken to reward, reset, or release, performance evaluation and feedback must occur.

Performance feedback is a major component of leadership action. Most organizations of any size have some sort of formal evaluation process that is used by the leaders to facilitate this important leadership function. I personally have accrued a stack of formal evaluations going back decades. To be honest, though, they were only marginally effective at helping me improve my performance. I was usually uncomfortable in the performance evaluation sessions. In part, it was because the evaluator nearly always seemed uneasy. The performance objectives were usually broad and my ability to achieve them was impacted by many factors outside my control. The expectations for which I was being evaluated were often unclear at the start of the evaluation timeframe and usually I had received very little feedback during the evaluation period. Also, no matter how good the review, there were always one or two items in the review that I would be told I needed to work on. I came to believe this was a standard practice—*"There's always room for improvement,"* as the expression goes—based on the belief that if a person is told their performance is optimal, they will lose all incentive to continue developing instead of reaching for new challenges. It all seemed so political rather than an honest person-to-person talk about my performance. Continual improvement is essential to stay competitive, but it must be framed in the context of a new challenge with an attainable goal. In other words, create a win-win, as Stephen Covey would say.

I sometimes doubted my leader's motives, wondering if there was a hidden agenda to serve his interests at the expense of mine.

This feeling was once validated when I transferred from one department to another in a company. I had received very good reviews in the old department. So good, in fact, that I was rewarded with the opportunity to move to a better position in a new department when a position opened. When it came time for my review I had been in the new department only a few months, so it was decided that the previous department head would do my review since I had spent more of the period working for him. Suddenly, his opinion of my work wasn't as good as it had been when I was reporting to him. It took a while for me to figure it out, because I am not a generally devious kind of person. I finally reasoned that the not-as-good review my former boss gave me would show his manager that he was willing to be tough and not just sugar coat the reviews (giving someone a performance review they won't like is hard for most leaders.) In other words, I believed his political agenda to advance his own career influenced him to give me a less than honest review. It was pretty easy for me to think this because I had known him to lie to get what he wanted and he was always figuring some angle to advance his interests. As General Colin Powell states, "Trust is the essence of leadership." Once a leader loses the trust of followers, many of his actions become suspect.

Formal performance appraisals *are* important to provide a record of feedback and to allow human resources and others to have a consistent framework for important organizational considerations like consistency and adherence to ethical and legal requirements. However, these formal feedback systems used alone will not create great performance.

Day-to-day feedback based on openness and trust holds more value for most people. Unfortunately, regular and open feedback based on mutual respect seems to be elusive in many organizations. The best leaders seem to be able to combine the formal evaluation and the skillful day-to-day informal feedback needed to create an open, honest, and respectful working relationship with their followers. *Failure* to provide feedback to followers can lead to unnecessary future conflict because...

Nature Abhors a Vacuum

This observation by Aristotle was about his understanding of physics at the time, but has taken on the modern meaning that "unfilled spaces tend to get filled." This is certainly true when a feedback vacuum exists. The person who is not getting regular feedback from his leader will make up something to fill the void. This can go one of two ways. He may develop an inflated sense of how well he is doing. In this scenario, conflict is certain when the opinion of the leader doesn't jive with how good the follower thinks he is doing and eventually the leader is forced to take some corrective action the follower thinks is unwarranted. This is seen played out on the TV show *America's Got Talent* when a person who believes he is a great performer is given negative feedback by the judges and audience. The negative feedback elicits shock, anger, and disbelief. The judges may even be criticized by the contestant. Apparently the contestant hasn't received much honest feedback about his abilities. Conversely, some folks who are doing a good job doubt their performance if no one ever praises them or comments on their good work. Of course, after some amount of time with no feedback, people may move into the "I guess it doesn't matter" zone, where the potential for declining performance is greater. All of these scenarios are undesirable. So what are some reasons people don't get performance feedback?

Can't We All Just Get Along?

One of the barriers to giving feedback is that most people (and yes, leaders are people, too) want to get along with other people. That in itself is a good thing, right? As a matter of fact, getting along well enough to cooperate is the basis for civilization. In order to achieve this harmony, many times we can just ignore the actions of others because we are not really affected. If we see someone doing something that has potentially bad results for them or others, we may choose to avoid conflict. If the person is a close friend or loved one, perhaps we will feel obligated to give him some feedback because we care about his welfare, but we still have the option of ignoring. A leader, however, does not have the luxury of ignoring very much if he is to be effective. Problems, including unacceptable performance, must be addressed, not only because ignoring poor performance can have immediate undesirable results, but also because a lack of action can be viewed as consenting to the low performance or unacceptable behavior, thus perpetuating it.

Silence is consent. An example of how silence can become consent is when a leader views someone committing an unsafe act like not locking out a piece of equipment before reaching in to clear a jam or make an adjustment. If the leader ignores the unsafe act, then the follower thinks it is okay because he doesn't understand the risk or he thinks the risk is acceptable to the boss. Now he feels okay committing that unsafe act in the future, thus increasing the likelihood that an accident will occur. It is easy to see how this failure to give performance feedback can result in a declining safety performance standard. The best leadership action would be to stop the unsafe act and then engage the employee about why it is unsafe and unacceptable, thus preventing recurrence. However, just finding things wrong and being good at communicating feedback is not good enough to create the best environment for working with and influencing people.

> **"Your silence gives consent."**
> **PLATO**

If a leader is just continually looking for things that are wrong and correcting the follower, then the follower can become defensive or paralyzed, losing self-confidence. Thus, their performance may actually worsen—just the opposite of what the leader wants. Some people will react to constant criticism by always being on guard. Others will only do what they feel they must do to preserve their job, reasoning: *"Why do anything if everything is wrong?"* While taking action to correct undesirable performance or behavior is essential to leadership, a leader must use a balanced approach, giving feedback about things that are going right as well as things that need to be changed. Truthfully, more is done that is right than wrong, yet there is a propensity to focus on the negative. We are unwittingly trained to do that. What gets the most attention—a good grade at school, or a failing grade? What gets attention on the news—the billions of human daily interactions that went smoothly, or the time that someone flipped out and did something ugly?

Extra effort to focus on the good work that a follower is doing and letting them know you noticed is very important to maintaining a positive balance in what leadership guru Stephen Covey calls "the emotional bank account," where positive and negative input from others is stored and becomes a major determinant in the quality of the relationship. If lots of positives have been deposited, then when negative feedback is required, a good overall relationship can still be maintained. Building a habit of making emotional bank account deposits really improves the quality of work life for everyone.

Evaluation and feedback—be it positive or negative—is necessary to maintain and improve organizational performance.

> "Compliments cost nothing, yet many pay dear for them."
>
> **THOMAS FULLER**

So, What Are You Gonna Do About It?

Let's suppose a leader has examined a follower's performance objectively. One can think of followers performing at one of three levels: exceptionally, adequately, or inadequately. Of course, within each of these categories there is a range and people can move around in that range. Be careful not to "pigeon hole" people by assuming they will always perform at the level you see at any given instant. It is also important to realize that poor performance in certain aspects of their job may be offset by really great performance in other areas. Overall, though, most people will fall into the adequate middle section. A few will be exceptional performers and a few will be performing unacceptably. I came to believe that the 80/20 distribution described by Vilfredo Pareto (also known as the "Pareto principle") worked pretty well for framing the three performance categories.

Eighty percent of people are in that vast adequately performing middle area; they simply want to do their job up to expectations and go home at the end of the day, ready to enjoy the rest of their lives. They may need a performance reminder now and then or expectations may need to be clarified when the leader notices performance slipping. Overall, though, they do their job well and will continue to do so if given feedback.

A few exceptional people comprise the top ten percent and are driven to high performance for a variety of reasons. They will go the extra mile to do more. These people are the ones who will step up and make sure things happen even if supervisors or managers are not present. It has been said that the true measure of leadership is what happens when the leader is not there.

Also, in every organization, there are a few people—represented by the bottom ten per cent—who struggle to perform adequately, whether it is due to lack of skill or just not caring. This group can burn up an inordinate amount of the leaders' time and energy. If that becomes the case, this lopsided expenditure of leadership energy can have a very negative effect on the organization.

In order to keep improving the performance of the organization, it is vital that leaders give ongoing feedback to *all* followers about their performance. Based on an objective evaluation of performance, a leader needs to take action. If the follower is meeting or exceeding expectations, they need to know it and be rewarded for it. If the follower is not meeting expectations, then it is time for the leader to review whether he has facilitated the work, developed a sense of ownership in the follower, and achieved understanding with the follower. If these prerequisites to performance are not in place, then the leader must put them in place. This process I call *resetting*. Maybe they didn't get it when you gave them ownership because they didn't understand or believe you. Maybe they didn't have everything they needed to do their work. In other words, the leader must consider how effective his own work has been; if it wasn't good enough, have a do-over. If the prerequisite fundamentals are in place, yet the follower still is unable or unwilling to improve performance, then the leader must release them to other pursuits. This does not necessarily mean dismissal. Sometimes people are willing to learn to improve their performance, but just don't have the talent needed. Maybe they got in over their head. They may perform admirably in another position. Great leaders discern the difference between people who can't perform in a particular position, but can still be an asset to the organization, and those who will continue to be a liability.

A very successful Vice President for a large corporation, Laura Folse, looks for the disconnect between what the person wants and what he is getting out of his work. "I sit down with them," Laura explained, "and I try to find a way to help them get the satisfaction they need in their work, or to bring something to their work that will give them satisfaction" (Abrashoff, 2004, p. 137). Sometimes, though, she winds up giving them another assignment or letting them go (releasing them). Not all leaders are as good. Here's a real life example of someone who wasn't as strong as Laura.

When You Have a Good Horse, You Ride It

The leader of a manufacturing plant where I once worked had an interesting approach to handling people. I once read an overview he gave the supervisors and managers about his philosophy right after he took the job. One thing he wrote stood out for me. He stated that he would *demand* more from his high performers. Continually improving performance *is* necessary to remain competitive, so on the surface this philosophy seems like a good guiding principle for a leader. I guess that would have been okay if he had been willing to address the low performers as well.

Instead, inadequate performers were shifted from job to job until they finally landed in a position with little responsibility and where I suppose he hoped they would do the least damage. He did, however, prove true to his philosophy of demanding more from high performers. I came to label this philosophy: "When You Have a Good Horse, You Ride It." The problem is the good horse can get an attitude if he is being ridden to exhaustion while the nags are lollygagging around in the stable. If the good horse is pushed to the point of exhaustion frequently because the rider can't rely on the nags to get him where he wants to go, he may then become so worn out that he just can't go like he used to, or he may refuse to run so hard in order to preserve himself. The good horse may also decide to jump the corral fence and seek greener pastures. If the good horse breaks and runs or becomes less effective due to overuse, the master has one less good horse and still has the same amount of no-good horses. One can easily see how the best organizational performance is not obtained by ignoring the low performers. All the performers must be attended to, whether they are exceptional, adequate, or inadequate. In addition to addressing low performance, what further can be done to promote and sustain high performance?

Rewarding Followers

If people perform well, they must be rewarded in order to maintain the good performance. If rewards (gains) are not forthcoming, organizational performance can begin to slip. There is the clear arrangement of monetary compensation that is a reward. The problem with this reward is that it is often taken for granted after some time. When I was a young supervisor, I saw clearly how the paycheck begins to lose its power to motivate after a while.

The second shift at the whiskey barrel plant where I worked had been discontinued for about a year when the demand for barrels by our parent distillery increased sufficiently to restart second shift. So, as a new foreman, it became my job to start up and supervise production on the added shift. Many of the needed workers would be recalled from layoff. This was long before the extended unemployment benefits of today that can last up to two years, so most of the displaced workers had taken lower paying jobs and were glad to get back to work at the cooperage. They were excited to earn the higher wages and grateful to be back. These experienced workers jumped right in and required minimal supervision from me. They seemed highly motivated, even helping to train the new hires. I didn't realize the honeymoon wouldn't last, and since I was inexperienced, I didn't take the necessary action to help safeguard their high spirits. After about six months, complaints began to increase and performance started declining. I have reflected on that phenomenon a lot over the years and determined that the decline of morale and performance were the result of a more or less human

63

nature to take things for granted... combined with the fact that I wasn't a very good supervisor. The recalled workers were no longer highly motivated by the paycheck and I wasn't giving them rewards that could replace that initial surge of gratefulness and motivation. How could I have helped keep their spirits up?

Step Right Up, Everyone's a Winner

The familiar carnival game barker's exhortation belies our natural desire to be a winner. We all want to be winners. Competition and the natural desire to win are deeply ingrained in our psyche. From childhood we compete for our parents' attention, peer approval, riding shotgun in the car (that could be a Southern thing), getting the girl or boy, getting good grades, the coolest ride, and on and on. As a result of this competition, people have a tendency to see themselves as winners or losers in various categories. The rewards we seek and receive in life we view as emblems of winning. It is really the feeling of winning that we are seeking, although we may enjoy the big house, the nice car, and other material things we earn (win), it is really the feeling we want more than anything. The same is true for awards, educational achievements, and praise from others.

Psychologist Abraham Maslow developed a hierarchy of needs that motivate people. At the very bottom of the list are food, sleep, shelter, sex, and such that meet the basic biological function needs. At the top is self-actualization and transcendence. In the middle, where most of us spend most of our efforts, are things like relationships, work groups, status, and achievement. Since most people in our wonderful country have their lowest level needs more or less met (according to Maslow's scale), they are more motivated by the psychological needs like achievement, status, self-esteem, etc. The more a leader can help followers meet those needs and achieve that feeling of winning and self-esteem, the more they will accept his influence. Powerful leaders come to know what constitutes a "win" for their followers. Even though credible praise, recognition, and material rewards seem to be universal wins for most people, each follower is different, and a win for one may not be so appreciated by another. Some folks may feel tremendously rewarded by public recognition. Others may feel more like a winner if they simply get some private recognition for their efforts. That is one of the reasons that developing open communication and a trust-based relationship is so important to serving up great leadership. A leader can then come to understand the wins that are important to each follower and help them reach those personal goals. That kicks leadership in to high gear, because it creates the "win/win" relationship that author Stephen Covey listed as one of the "seven habits of highly effective people."

A Winning Team

While on the subject of rewards, I think a word about team rewards is important. Organizational effectiveness is dependent on teamwork more than ever before. Even someone who seems to be rewarded by solely their own efforts, like commissioned salespeople, or workers who get paid by the number of widgets they produce are dependent on others for their performance. Interdependence is ever increasing in modern life. That means individual performance is greatly affected by the performance of others in the organization and vice versa. This is readily apparent in most manufacturing settings where a single bottleneck can affect dozens or hundreds of workers.

Think of an auto assembly line. If the line stops due to a single work station not operating correctly, things back up pretty quickly, impacting the entire line. Therefore, it is important to note and reward team effort and to reward individuals for helping the team when there may not be a direct benefit to them. In order to promote teamwork, when I would see someone going out of their way to help a new employee or help someone on the team that was having a bad day, I would be sure to thank them for it. If a team had a really good day, I would sometimes ask my boss to stop by and congratulate them. If financial incentives can be set up to reward teams, so much the better. That can be tricky business, though, and if not carefully planned can become a disincentive to folks who feel they are unfairly left out. Individual leaders can reward teams in a lot of ways, though. I have rewarded teams with something as simple and inexpensive as providing ice cream and cookies at break time or bringing in donuts the day following an outstanding achievement. The little things count for a lot.

Correcting Course – Resetting

Just as when the captain of a ship at sea determines the vessel has strayed from its course and he must take action to correct the course, when a leader finds the performance of a follower is not meeting expectations, action is required. Although most leaders don't expend enough effort rewarding followers, it is also true that leaders often let unacceptable performance continue for way too long. This low performance typically doesn't just go away, and it isn't going to get any easier to deal with as time goes on. If an employee has been allowed to continue in low performance for a long time then it will be much more difficult to deal with when things get so bad that something *must* be done.

Let's say someone has been in a position for a few years performing at a very low level, but no one has really dealt with the issue. Now, when action must be taken, the employee will be very upset because they have rationalized that their performance must be okay since nothing has happened in all this time. They will be resistant to accepting this new view of their performance and may take some action to defend their ego, like grievances or other action that prompts third party reviews. When the third party starts examining the validity of the leader's action, they will be interested in any previous attempts by the leaders to improve performance. If they find nothing to indicate that the employee has been given opportunities to correct their performance, they are going to be much more likely to mitigate or reverse the leader's action, damaging the leader's credibility. That is a good reason to document actions, even if just in the form of daily notes, or planner and journal entries. Here are some ideas to help you be effective when resetting expectations.

The Four C's of Constructive Feedback

Even though we have addressed performance evaluation and feedback, here is a good place to look more specifically at how to give *constructive* feedback. Sometimes this kind of feedback is referred to as negative feedback. The difference is that constructive feedback provides a positive element to providing input toward achieving desired performance. Negative feedback, without the positive improvement component, runs the risk of leaving the receiver feeling insulted, inadequate, or unclear about what must be done to improve. Giving *constructive* feedback requires:

Commitment – A leader must know why he is willing to do the hard stuff others are not willing to do. Motives may include a strong work ethic with a sense that *It is my job, so I'll just do it*, a desire to make the world better, a desire to advance one's own career, or a combination of these factors. Knowing "why" to do it leads to commitment.

Courage–Commitment leads to developing the courage to give feedback, knowing conflict may occur. Even though

> "Just do what must be done. This may not be happiness, but it is greatness."
> **GEORGE BERNARD SHAW**

conflict can result in improvement, it can be stressful, particularly when not handled well. Studying conflict styles and conflict management can really be helpful in bolstering courage to give constructive feedback. Courage is also needed to "seek first to understand" and to have the humility to be wrong when new facts are presented during feedback.

Consideration – This is the willingness to regard the human side of the person receiving the feedback; it includes empathy and compassion.

Conciseness – A leader must learn to be concise when delivering feedback. It is natural to be nervous when giving any feedback that could be viewed as negative, but don't ramble. Usually the receiver of the feedback is highly sensitized when it becomes apparent that he is being corrected and then every word is scrutinized. Unnecessary words then become opportunities for debate and defense. For example, if a leader observes an unsafe act and responds with corrective action, he can deliver this to a follower by: (1) "I am aware that you disregarded company safety rules and…" or (2) "I noticed that you… [did so-and-so]… and that is unsafe." The words "disregarded company safety rules" are unnecessary and imply willful noncompliance, though that may not be the case. In response, the employee may become defensive and now a communication barrier is in place that makes it more difficult to reach agreement about changing the unsafe behavior. Stick to the facts.

Let There Be Silence

Silence is a useful technique when resetting expectations. Open a dialogue by stating what you have observed that you believe is a problem, how it affects organizational performance, and any other pertinent facts, then be silent. Even though you may think you have all the facts and even a solution to the problem, let the other person respond. It is powerful when you give them space. They may tell you something you don't know about why the performance is not satisfactory. Maybe you thought they had everything they needed to do the work, but they didn't. It is amazing what they may say. Sometimes they have been aware of the fact that they need to improve but had just let other things get in the way and will offer to make improvements once they realize it is going to be dealt with. Of course, it's not always that easy. Sometimes they will try to game you by diverting attention to the performance of others or even your own performance. (Let's assume your own lack of performance isn't the reason they haven't performed and it is only a diversionary tactic). Stay on track by restating the problem you have observed. Don't engage in an argument. Remember, this is about performance, not the person. Let the silence work for you. If the situation becomes too emotional or heated, it may be best to call a time-out, with the clear expectation that the discussion will continue after a "cooling off" period. This may require you to take charge to prevent the situation from getting out of hand. Use your positional authority only as needed.

In the end, though, there must be some agreement about how to correct the performance. Solicit their ideas about how to do that and together develop a plan that has measurable goals. Let them know it is *their* responsibility to improve and that you will assist them if you can, but don't take on the monkey.

Don't Get Personal, Bub

So, how can a leader give necessary feedback without alienating the follower? By focusing on the issue, not the person. A leader must develop the skills to address issues without appearing to be *judgmental*, a word that has negative overtones and connotes personal judging. Avoid overuse of the personal pronoun *you*. Notice it is called a *personal* pronoun. How can they help but take anything that follows *you* personally. Instead of saying, "You are not getting the job done," one can say, "We are not getting the results we need. Can you see a way to improve?" Instead of saying, "You made a lot of mistakes in that report," it may be valuable to say, "I noticed several mistakes on the report. How can the accuracy be improved?" They already know they did the report. One approach seems accusatory. The other conveys the need for improvement without accusing.

The Performance is Not the Person

A really serious mistake a leader can make is to confuse the person with the performance. A person's inadequate performance doesn't lessen their value as a human being. When a leader is giving feedback, he must be careful to confine the feedback to professional performance. A confusion that can plague leaders and inhibit good working relationships is allowing performance failures to influence their view of a person's general worth as a human being. Just because a person performs very poorly in his or her job doesn't mean that they are an overall failure as a person and a leader must be careful to confine his judgments to the parameters of the relationship. Also, extraneous knowledge about their personal life should not influence feedback about job performance. It is not helpful to consider any of their personal failures when evaluating their job performance and they will certainly resent it if they think their personal life is being judged.

At this point some readers may be wondering, "Do leaders actually do this?" I'll answer that question with a question. Can you imagine a leader saying something like, "She is really messed up," or "That guy is a loser."? We are social creatures with egos that can cause us to want to perceive ourselves as "better than" others. Being able to control these very human traits, though, is part of being professional.

Personal activities outside work can, of course, affect job performance. This would include any substance abuse issues, run-ins with the law, and possibly other things. In the end, though, it is still about how individual performance—or the collective organization—is affected by those activities. It is not an opportunity for an ego boost by putting them down. Note: Good expert advice is needed when addressing such issues due to legal ramifications.

When address-ing performance issues, a great prin-ciple to follow is to *focus on the problem, not the person.*

> **"Focus on the problem, not the person."**

Release

Another necessary part of leadership is letting someone go when unacceptable performance or behavior dictates. It could mean separating someone from the organization or simply getting them into another position where they can perform acceptably.

Before we get too far into this subject, let's have a word about *words*. Words are important. Our choice of words affects our per-spective and our perspective influences our willingness to act. Words like *terminate* and *fire* promote fear. If someone is fired or terminated, it is as if their life will be negatively altered in such a way that who knows what might happen. They may lose their home, the kids won't go to college, or any manner of ill might be-fall them. All kinds of fears are conjured up.

Of course, if these kinds of events actually occur, they are never the result of a single action like being separated from current employ-ment. The leader who must take action is also fearful because there is risk that the action won't produce the desired result. The point is that this kind of action by a leader kicks fear into high gear and human beings tend to avoid the things they are afraid of. Effective leaders overcome the fear and make decisions that contain risk.

So, what can be done to decrease the fear? One thing is to change the perspective by using different language to describe the necessary action. That is why I say *release* instead of *fire* or *terminate*. But, am I just playing a word game? No, and let me explain.

It is not a kindness to refrain from transferring or separating someone when continued low performance or unacceptable behavior indicates such action. On the surface it may seem kind to keep them in their current position so they won't have to suffer any financial or

71

emotional pain, but a leader must consider the net effect on the individual and the organization. Short term pain may be required in order to make long term gains. From the organizational perspective, if a follower who is performing at a very low level is replaced with a higher performer, the result will be a higher performing organization. Then, all the individuals remaining in the organization will be better served by being part of a more effective and secure organization.

Group dynamics will be improved as well. Most jobs today are interdependent. The performance of Employee A affects the performance of Employees B and C. If Employee A improves, it presents the opportunity for B and C to improve. As an example, let's think about accuracy of reports. If a report contains inaccuracies, people who rely on the information in the report may make bad decisions based on the incorrect information. When the report accuracy is improved by a higher performer, the people who use that report can do a better job.

> "Leadership is, among other things, the ability to inflict pain and get away with it - short-term pain for long-term gain."
>
> **GEORGE WILL**

Another dynamic involves the psychology of the workplace. Remember the story about how when you have a good horse, you ride it? When a leader takes action to correct low performance, the good horses notice and are motivated to continue their good performance. Some marginal performers may decide to consider improving their performance as well in order to avoid consequences. But what about the individual who is separated from their livelihood?

Best Thing That Ever Happened to Me

Besides being the title of a song that enjoyed popularity in several genres, those words have often been expressed by people who have been released from a job where they weren't performing well. Often low performers know they aren't quite up to snuff and it is taking a toll on them emotionally. I have encountered few people who just didn't care if they were getting the job done or not. Well then, you may ask, if a person knows he isn't performing well and is suffering from it, why doesn't he find a way to do something different? Our old friend Fear holds him back. A change could make things worse. Maybe he would like to do something different where he can perform better, but the great unknown is too scary. Aren't we all kind of like that? Empathize by asking yourself what has held you back from realizing your full potential. Then, assuming you have facilitated for him, provided a sense of ownership, and sought to understand, do what needs to be done to release him. Release him to new opportunities. Like Laura Folse, seek the win/win solution to improve organizational performance and let the follower move to a place where he can perform and get greater satisfaction. That is great leadership.

Don't Be a Lone Ranger

Even the smartest and best leaders don't try to go it alone when making decisions like releasing. They seek input from others. In most organizations, it is clear that human resources or other parties that know the legal ramifications of a leader's actions must be consulted before serious actions such as letting an employee go is taken by a leader. Even though releasing someone may be good for all in the end, it is still complicated, costly, and traumatic and shouldn't be taken lightly.

In my early years I thought it should be easy to fire someone, but as I matured as a leader, I came to understand that it should be hard to separate someone—because of the serious effects on both the organization and the individual. Thoughtful consideration and objective scrutiny are needed. Don't be like The Lone Ranger who only consulted with Tonto, his Native American sidekick, before taking the most severe action on those he labeled the "bad guys." Although the quick acting, always winning, independent action hero is lauded in popular fiction, leaders live in the real world.

Arbitrary action is seldom warranted and I *know* that method won't work well for today's leaders. Great leaders develop a network of trustworthy counselors who will give them honest feedback and then they make great decisions.

Achieving organizational objectives requires skillful leadership to evaluate performance objectively, provide feedback, and take action to *reward, reset* the components of facilitation, ownership, and understanding, or *release* the person if he can't or won't perform as needed. By attending to all followers, the leader creates an environment where folks can do their personal best, grow, and feel they contribute to organizational success.

Summary

Leadership requires attention to many details involved in influencing others toward specific objectives. Leaders must be keen to human psychology and must also guide followers in practical matters that pertain to objectives. Both emotional and cognitive intelligence are required. The myriad facets of human psychology and emotions alone can almost seem overwhelming; this person responds in one way to a certain input and another responds differently. Add the knowledge a   leader needs to help guide followers through everyday roadblocks to achieving organizational objectives and one can easily see how leaders can get bogged down in activities and personal exchanges that don't yield the desired results. That is why a simple and effective way of viewing fundamental leadership activities is helpful. Any activity can then be considered against the fundamentals of leadership to gauge how effective it will be in accomplishing goals.

The Four Fundamentals of Practical Leadership are an easy to remember set of principles that a leader can use to guide his daily actions to influence followers. The fundamentals provide a foundational way of thinking and acting that supports followers in pursuing organizational goals. These principles also guide leadership actions to maintain high performance. Finally, if remedial action is necessary to correct performance, a leader who practices the Four Fundamentals will do what is necessary while minimizing the downside results to both the organization and individuals.

When considering if individuals or groups are accomplishing what you want, ask yourself the following questions to determine if you are practicing the **FOUR Fundamentals of Practical Leadership**.

Facilitation – Do people have the time, materials, equipment, training, methods, and information they need to do what I have asked?

Ownership – Have I created a sense of ownership by applying gains and losses based on individual and group performance?

Understanding – Is there a high level of both cognitive and emotional understanding in the organization that is supported by a psychologically safe environment?

Reward, Reset, or Release – Am I acting to reward desirable performance? Do I need to review and reset facilitation, ownership, and understanding to improve performance? Is it time to release the person that is not going to perform satisfactorily?

Learning and practicing the Four Fundamentals of Practical Leadership will build a strong foundation that can support an individual's leadership journey throughout a lifetime. The results will include greater job satisfaction, a more positive work environment, greater efficiency, less stress, higher organizational performance, and career opportunity enhancement. Developing great leadership skills can make an awesome difference in the quality of life for both leaders and followers and make the world a better place where leaders and followers work together to achieve worthy goals in an atmosphere of mutual respect. Sounds like pretty lofty stuff, doesn't it? The high calling of leadership can make it happen when leaders practice the Four Fundamentals of Practical Leadership. May blessings be upon you throughout your leadership journey.

Suggested Reading

Abrashoff, D. Michael. (2004). *Get Your Ship Together: How Great Leaders Inspire Ownership from the Keel Up.* New York: Penguin Group.

Ambrose, Stephen E. (1998). *The Victors: Eisenhower and His Boys: The Men of World War II.* New York: Simon & Schuster.

Covey, Stephen R. (1989). *The 7 Habits of Highly Effective People: Powerful Lessons in Personal Change.* New York: Fireside.

Fournies, Ferdinand F. (2007). *Why Employees Don't Do What They're Supposed To and What You Can Do About It.* New York: McGraw-Hill.

Maslow, Abraham. (1954). *Motivation and Personality.* New York: Harper.

Massey, Morris. (2006). *What You Are Is Where You Were When... AGAIN!* Cambridge, MA: Enterprise Media. [Training video available at www.enterprisemedia.com/product/00125/what-you-are-is-where-you-were-when-again]

Maxwell, John C. (2007). *The 21 Irrefutable Laws of Leadership: Follow Them and People Will Follow You.* Nashville, TN: Thomas Nelson, Inc.

Sowell, Thomas. (2007). *Basic Economics: A Common Sense Guide to the Economy.* New York: Basic Books.

Sullivan, Robert I. (2010). *Good Boss, Bad Boss: How to Be the Best... and Learn from the Worst.* New York: Business Plus.

www.ingramcontent.com/pod-product-compliance
Lightning Source LLC
Chambersburg PA
CBHW071245170526
45165CB00003B/1247